THE EXTROVERT'S SURVIVAL GUIDE

Debra Yergen

Whole House Publications
S·E·A·T·T·L·E

Debra Yergen

Dedicated to my mom, a genuine extrovert, who has never known a stranger, and my dad, an introvert who was captivated by mom on their first date more than 50 years ago.

Library of Congress. First Edition.

ISBN: 9798634060859

We hope you enjoy this book from Whole House Publications.

www.WholeHousePubs.com

Printed in the United States of America.

CONTENTS

FORWARD

by Dr. Raul Garcia,
Emergency Physician

What does it mean to be healthy?

Under usualcircumstances, it's everything patients discuss with their physicians. Diet. Exercise. Stress. A lack of sleep. Substance use, from caffeine to prescriptions, as well as ways to deal with their lifestyle routines and demands. Life can be chaotic and unfamiliar, especially during a pandemic. The healthiest people find a way to balance connecting physically, mentally, and spiritually.

Preparation and a commitment to consistently positive decision-making will serve a person well. But what about when that's not possible or not enough? Generally, when people fall physically ill, there's a point where they or someone else makes a necessary call for medical help. Unfortunately, when people are suffering with stress, anxiety, or another mental health crisis, asking for help is more difficult. Depression can be a   silent struggle and can be deadly.

As an Emergency Physician, I've treated hundreds of patients with COVID-19, with a range of symptoms from mild to severe. Circumstances, hormones, and disease can all trigger chemical responses. Everyone experiences bouts of physical and mental health distress, and everyone experiences them differently.

Sometimes prevention is not enough, but the good news is that help is available.

In the Emergency Department, there are different levels of response teams. A response to a broken arm will be different than a response to a heart attack or trauma. COVID-19, and the worldwide response to it, has changed the way we live and react to daily activities. Life coaching best practices are valuable for many people in regaining control of your life surrounded by so much change. But if you need a different level of care or response to your situation, seek help.

If you are feeling overwhelmed for several days or weeks, or having thoughts of harming yourself or others, talk to a counselor, healthcare provider or clergy immediately. No one is going to judge you. Help is available, through your local medical community, and through national organizations like the National Alliance on Mental Illness (NAMI). Find local resources at NAMI.org or call the national NAMI hotline at 800-950-NAMI (6264).

INTRODUCTION

There are many good reasons to hibernate indoors, away from family, friends, and of course acquaintances this fall and winter. If you live in a cold climate, or a region with four seasons, winter may be a good reason to stay indoors. When it's cold and wet or icy, it's normal to seek the comfort of a fireplace or cozy blanket and something warm to drink. Health reasons are also a good reason to maintain a safe distance. For those who are immune-system compromised are safer giving themselves some distance from others, especially in flu season. And of course there is COVID-19. That dreaded virus that took over the world in 2020.

Everyone is tired of it. We thought it would be weeks, and now nine months later it's still here and looking to share an encore performance. Avoiding it, denying it and ignoring it is not going to make it go away. We know what we need to do by this point. If only someone had fresh ideas about tips, recipes, and activities to help our kids, friends and ourselves. Great news! The Extrovert's Survival Guide is for you! It includes months worth of fresh ideas to get your family through a second wave of COVID-19, from nurses, teachers, and an essential oil expert.

Although the term social distancing has only been around for a short time, the virus that sparked it, COVID-19, and the way it has completely changed the world, is emotionally, mentally, socially, and spiritually attacking extroverts (and many introverts) in a way this generation has never experienced. Maintaining a safe physical distance from others has been labeled social distancing, when in fact, social distancing is harmful. People need people. Viruses require physical distancing, not giving up the connections that feed our souls.

My coaching clients and friends alike used words like dark, lonely, crying, exhausted, guilty, depressed and references to feeling like they are "going to die." Not from COVID-19 – but rather from "social distancing." For them, the early steps toward physical isolation intended to help stop a killer virus equated to social starvation. Glued to their televisions or computers, many reported saturating themselves with conflicting reports of the signs of this world pandemic. Most people struggled, but self-described extroverts (people who renew their energy from others) reported screaming for help, hugs, and social interaction.

Summer was a turning point. Masks became required in most places, to prevent even non-symptomatic people from inadvertently spreading the virus. But what many people felt they lost in freedom, they made up for in businesses reopening. With precautions, as a society, we were able to dine out, meet in small, physically distanced groups, indulge in farmer's markets and U-pick farms, and even attend church services and in some cases school.

Experts told us not to get too comfortable. It turns

out the scientists and epidemiologists were right about a second round. The last time we "hunkered down" in March and early April, people got restless quickly. While most people have become experts at knowing what to do, the same activities and apps have grown stale. That's why this survival guide is packed with a whole new set of COVID-19 tips and tricks. This is not going away in a few weeks, but you're ahead of the game. You've stumbled across a survival guide to breathe new life and variety into your routine.

Physical distancing drives down exposure and viral spread. Physical distancing drives protection, while social distancing drives isolation.

Ready for some good news? This compact survival guide includes help, hope and a section listing a month's worth of creative things anyone can do today to connect with others, while respecting physical distancing and staying safe! It's like having your own life coach, prompting you with questions. **You decide what feels best to you right now.**

You may wonder: what are life coaches? Life coaches are not physicians, therapists, counselors, or friends.

Life coaches are trained with a set of tools and best practices to help you find and voice your own answers. This is a coaching survival guide for people who have had their normal way of life turned upside down and are trying to figure out how to regain a sense of joy.

You already have the answers. On the following pages, I'll help you access them.

I invited my good friend, Dr. Raul Garcia, an emergency physician, to write the forward and join the media tour for this survival guide because the physical and mental impact of isolation and change is real. Dr. Garcia is someone I seek the counsel of when I have medical questions (physical and mental health questions) that extend beyond life coaching practices.

Our minds are powerful, and we can achieve a great deal with intention, determination, goals, and a plan to get there. But sometimes, sudden change can be overwhelming, and we need medical help. Asking for help is a sign of strength. Learning new skills is a sign of resilience. And helping and accepting help from others is a sign of community and belonging.

Let's all band together to be strong, resilient and filled with a sense of community and belonging as we finish out 2020 and jump into 2021 knowing the best is yet to come.

LESSON ONE

It's Healthy to Ask for Help

Extroverts are people who need people.

We all need other people, but some people need regular interactions more than others. Some people recharge, refuel, reenergize, and come alive when they are among friends and strangers. For people like this, social isolation can feel suffocating, like a wet blanket over a campfire.

If you're not a healthcare provider or essential employee, staying home is about far more than the perk of sleeping in an extra 30 minutes, or trading your commute for a morning walk. And if you're a parent with school-age children, you're now juggling your routine and possibly theirs, all while working from home or working to take care of your home. For parents who are home schooling for the first time, it turns out that teaching fractions and equations is a lot harder than doubling a cake recipe.

Getting ready from the waist up requires less effort and delivers greater comfort for those conducting business on Zoom, Google Meets, TEAMS, Skype, Facebook

Live, Marco Polo, and well, you get the idea. But for many, the consequences outweigh the benefits. (Just try opening the door to any delivery driver half dressed and you both may wish you had finished getting dressed.)

The financial crisis that has accompanied this pandemic is hitting small businesses in a life-shattering way. Approximately a third of the United States is furloughed, out of work, or underemployed, and the longer it takes to get the virus under control, the more devastating that becomes.

As if all of this isn't enough, the emotional and mental tolls of isolation can be deafening.

Most wish 2020 would hurry up and pass on by. But before getting rid of 2020 becomes *the action plan*, consider the celebrations on December 31, 2019, when no one could have imagined the chaos the new decade would hold. We don't know what lies ahead in 2021. We don't even know what lies ahead tomorrow.

The good news is that there's hope, and there's help. By the time you finish this short survival guide, you'll have the tools and a solid plan to thrive. Even better, you'll be able to use these same exercises to address any future challenge regardless of what it stems from or what the cause.

Before we get there, let's start with where we're at.

The actions we refer to as social distancing have changed everything.

- *"I don't recognize myself. My hair is gray. My feet look terrible. I look in the mirror and I don't want anyone to see me this way, especially on a video conference.*

> *Who's this woman? This isn't me,"* a client told me as she sniffled through the phone.

- *"Forget the virus, I'm going to die here in my own home from complete isolation,"* another woman wrote on Twitter.
- *"If I go out to buy something, I feel bad. If I stay in, I feel trapped, like a wild animal in a cage,"* wrote another.
- *"I'm lonely. I have such dark thoughts. I don't have any desire to get up, shower, shave, or eat because what's the point?"* one man said to me in a phone call.

These examples are real, and they are a fraction of the cries for help that I've heard this year. **People from all walks of life are searching to make sense of their circumstances and create a thriving new normal.**

The good news: It's our choice. Either we learn and grow, or we let uncertainty and chaos take us down. At Olive Press Coaching, we have a saying: **How will you show up?** Most of us don't have the luxury of changing the world to fit us, but we do get to decide if we show up and if so, how we show up. Do we show up frustrated and angry, or accepting and open? Do we grumble or do we exercise our power to decide?

As an introvert, I do not truly understand the feelings of an extrovert. But I listen and I use tools that are proven to help anyone achieve their goals if they are willing to do the work.

When it comes to life coaching, it's all about choice. Your choice, to decide what you want and how you will show up.

ACTIVITY:

Think about yourself under normal circumstances. Which of these words resonate with your life before COVID-19 impacted your community and world? You can put a check by them or mentally note them.

Social butterfly

Active in the community

Fun and enjoys talking through ideas

Busy and thriving

Involved in activities

Making people laugh

Gathering friends

Solving problems

Surrounded by people

Reveling in friendly competition

How do you feel reading this list? What happens if you read this list again and for each one, remember a time when you felt these feelings? When was the last time you felt active in your community, busy and thriving or reveling in friendly competition? Creating this imagery may not give you the sense of fullness equal to enjoying a meal, but it can provide some nourishment.

It may even provide enough energy and joy to get through this coaching lesson and implement activities that will rejuvenate your spirit back to feeling like yourself again. **Read the list one more time and name at last one person who was present at a time when you experienced each of these memories.** Why are you doing this? Because every time you conjure up positive feelings associated with good memories, it will fuel feelings of connected-ness.

What is social isolation like for extroverts?

This post grabbed my attention on Facebook. It grabbed a lot of attention with most people agreeing: *"Just sank in this year no Easter celebration. My kids can't come over. it will be just me and my hubby. I will find a way to find the bless-ings, but right now my heart aches and I'm mad at the people who continue to have people over or are out clearly not adhering to the social distancing. Getting people to come to your house to work out if your personal trainer is not available is not social distancing. Going to cut people's hair at their house is not social distancing. You should only be around the person (people) you live with 24/7. That's it and that could change too, if they get sick or you get sick. The people who continue to ignore this are making hell on earth because of their selfishness. I'm watching my fellow nurses work their butts off, crying every day. They too are scared they're gonna bring COVID-19 home.*

How many times do we have to keep saying it: STAY HOME! All you have to do is stay home."

Everyone suffers, but for extroverts, it's more. Social isolation is a war on your nature and happiness. And when people are at war, they either turn the energy in-ward (and let emotions and stress eat away at them) or out toward others, especially those who are violating social norms. It shares similarities to someone surviving with-out sleep.

After a period of no sleep, or prolonged inadequate sleep, a person's body will sometimes collapse because they are so tired and need to recharge.

If you are an extrovert, you need to recharge your

energy. You need your people and your social normalcy to feel energized again. That can feel impossible in an environment of social distancing.

For people who are hitting breaking points, there are only two ways to respond. Either you respond in a way that breaks you down, or you respond in a way that builds you up.

This survival guide provides you with the tools to create a plan to claim control of your life. Either you control your life, or you lose control and either violate social norms and put yourself or others at risk, or internalize the pain and melt into worry, frustration, stress, pain, and anxiety. **The activities in this short survival guide will help you take control of your choices**. This coaching tool will help you recharge in a healthy and natural way that empowers you to reclaim your joy and ability to connect with your world.

LESSON TWO

Get Out of Your Head

Extroverts are doers. Sometimes they think about the consequences of what they do and sometimes they just do what seems natural, but rarely, under normal conditions do you hear of extroverts snuggling up on their sofa alone recharging. If you are an extrovert, you may be thinking, *"I would only do that if I was sick, and I'm never sick."*

Extroverts are the great information gatherers and sharers. If you want to learn unusual facts or find out what is going on, visit the social media page of an extrovert. Many of them find the action, take pictures, and sprinkle those photos everywhere like confetti. Surely it was an extrovert who first said, *"The more the merrier."*

Over-thinking life is traditionally associated with introverts, while their opposite extrovert friends don't have time for over-thinking. They are out finding or creating something to do and doing it. With COVID-19, this dynamic has almost completely flipped.

Trapped in their homes, extroverts are not just going stir-crazy. They are losing themselves without the ability to recharge their fun, happy, social batteries. (There are introverts who are also feeling anxious by social distancing, especially if they live with extroverts who are climbing the walls and driving them nuts.)

"I try to stay home, even though it's killing me. I want to go out, for a few things, but then I consider that I've gone through all of this and all it takes is one wrong exposure to the virus and all of this was for nothing. And that makes me feel very afraid," Brian, an extrovert shared in April. (To be fair, warm summer months have given responsible extroverts the opportunity to meet for drinks, in a large backyard, social distancing, and fulfilling the need to see friends and hear voices without using technology. Winter is coming, and without a vaccine, those who live in colder climates could once again find themselves physically isolated and emotionally starved.

ACTIVITY:

In a coaching situation, we do not deal with a client's psychological barriers or feelings. Instead, we acknowledge feelings, and ask questions that lead to a plan to move forward from stagnation to thriving success. Some of the questions might include:

What do you ultimately want to create? What is your end goal?

Let's brainstorm. There's no wrong answer.

1. Imagine what your happiness looks like.
2. Write down everything you can think of that describes the picture of happiness in your mind.
3. Keep listing. Extroverts are not natural list-

makers, so just try to push yourself beyond your comfort zone. List as many things as you can before your minds feels restless. These can be thoughts, memories or anything that makes you feel social, happy, and thriving. (If this makes you uncomfortable writing these down, you may want to call a close friend and talk through them.)

4. The goal is to get these out of your head so you can stop thinking and start doing. If you're sub-consciously feeling stuck, this will nudge you for-ward.

It's okay if you come back to your list over the course of hours or days. The goal is to move your mind to thinking about things that make you happy, and that make you feel connected to your world again. Before you start your list, give yourself permission to set it down at any time. In bold, block letters, write at the top of the page: THINGS THAT MAKE ME HAPPY! Every day add at least one new item to your list. The more detail, the better.

It's okay if throughout your list-making day(s), you sometimes, feel guilty or overwhelmed. That's a natural setback. But each time you find yourself returning to your head, follow that by returning to your happiness list and add something else to it. You are a doer, and this is prep-ping you for success.

If the news and uncertainty of the world situ-ation surrounding COVID-19 make you feel discouraged, give yourself permission to daydream. Daydreaming about positive things can create positive emotions and help re-lease serotonin.

When you need to escape your emotions, visualize a situation, scenario or destination that would bring you great joy. It may be a vacation or a relationship. It may be spending time with those you love. It may be hugging a friend or loved one. It may be checking something off your bucket list. It can be anything you want or anything you want to feel.

A word of caution: if you focus intently on this activity, you very well may draw it to you in real life. This is a real exercise I work through with my coaching clients and it's incredibly powerful.

When the mind vividly imagines something, noting each detail with focused attention on the six senses, your mind and body subconsciously make decisions and take actions that will bridge the gap between your life today and the image in your mind. Notice the nuance. Mere imagery will not magically make your dreams come true. But if you want something enough, and you imagine it with enough detail to make it feel real, your mind and body will take the steps (you will do the work and make the choices) to move closer to the dream you imagine.

ACTIVITY:

Imagine, or even better, write down, how you envision your life to look 60 days from this moment. Where are you living? What are you doing? Are you working or volunteering? What does your home environment feel like? How are you feeling? Can you touch your environment? Do you have a garden? Can you reach down and run your fingers through the dirt? It's okay if you have gloves on, unless you want to feel the soft soil in your fingers. What scents surround you? Are you alone or with other people? Are you near friends? Are you attending a BBQ? Are you struggling to carry in a hostess gift and a side salad? Are you just happy to be reunited with dear ones?

As you look around, what do you see? What do you want to see? Do you see color? Do you see smiles? Do you see ladybugs or sunshine? Do you see yourself graduating from school or a program? Do you see yourself buying a house? Do you see yourself attending a sporting event? Do you see yourself receiving an award?

What do you hear? What do you wish you heard? Imagine you hear what you want to hear. How does that make you feel? Do you hear laugher, or singing? Do you hear the wind or waves? Do you hear children playing or a pet letting you know you are appreciated?

Do you have hopes and dreams? What are you doing to make those happen? How is your health? What are you doing to get or stay healthier? Close your eyes. Inhale and exhale six deep breaths. Your world is changing for the better. You have so much to look forward to. You have so much to feel good about. **Your life is going to be different 60 days from now. How do you want it to look?**

During May, when many people were figuratively climbing the walls, I posed this question on social media: *If you could have 24 hours to do whatever you wanted with no consequences, what would you do before returning to self-quarantine?*

The most common responses included:

- *I'd hug and kiss all my family members.*
- *I'd reserve a house at the beach (oceanfront) and gather my immediate family (there are 17 of us) and do all the stuff we enjoy doing together: cooking, beach combing, board games, bonfire, laughing, chasing toddlers, taking pictures, singing, and touring up and down the coast.*

- *I'd go shopping with my mom to different thrift stores.*
- *I'd go out singing karaoke and hiking with friends at Rocky Mountain National Park.*
- *I'd visit my partner who works in another state and currently unable to leave due to lockdown.*
- *I'd gather all my friends to shop and drive around, then go party, play, dance, and spoil our kids.*
- *I'd sit at my own table at a coffee shop, surrounded by other people.*
- *I'd hug everyone I know!*

How surprised are you that none of the responses included winning the lottery, buying a sports car, meeting a celebrity, or any major bucket list item? Every single response involved spending time with people, mostly the people dearest to them. COVID-19 has brought great pain in so many ways. But it's also brought great appreciation for what matters most.

LESSON THREE

Look Past the Trees to the Forest

What do you want?

That's a loaded question for anyone to be asked, but especially an extrovert, because an entire list of things often comes to mind. So, let's narrow that down. **What do you want your life to look and feel like under the current circumstances?**

Yes, of course you want your normal life and your normal routine back. And it will come. *Not Forever But For Now*, is the name of a book by child development expert and author, Heather Malley. That describes our global experience under COVID-19. So in the meantime, what do you really need to feel fed and whole (or closer to whole) in this moment?

One client described her daily life in isolation as a nightmare that was suffocating her. As a career woman who was very successful in a sales position that required her to travel, her state-imposed quarantine essentially grounded her at home. Additionally, with the schools closed, she had suddenly picked up home-schooling duties and a daily stint as what she called *the cafeteria lady*.

Her husband was also home, and while she was constantly disinfecting the house and managing the needs of the household, he was outside in his shop, enjoying his furlough time pursuing his woodworking hobby. While he frequently asked how he could help, his follow-through did not measure up to her expectations. So inevitably, she gave him permission to retreat to his workshop while she felt increasingly overwhelmed.

By the time she called me, she was ready to cry. While she continued to give love, support, meals, help and energy to everyone around her, she was not receiving what she needed to recharge. As one week rolled into the next, her normally bright, busy, joyful, boisterous spirit became increasingly depleted and dark.

Extroverts everywhere understand what it's like to get lost in the details of daily life without the opportunity to recharge.

Let me say that again. Extroverts everywhere understand what it's like to get lost in the details of daily life without the opportunity to recharge.

Are you happy? Are you struggling? It's okay if you don't know.

As a certified life coach, I was trained by a company called iPEC. They have some awesome tools and concepts that are based on best practices. I use many of their fundamentals in helping my clients discover how to reclaim their joy and purpose. In my practice, I use a version of the iPEC Wheel of Life that I received in my training from them. I've adapted it into a list below.

I'm going to tell you a secret. It's often the area of life you least expect that's dragging down every other area. And that's GREAT NEWS because it means that with a little tweaking, you can reclaim your happiness much more quickly than you might think.

ACTIVITY:

Rate the following areas of your life from 1 to 10, with 1 meaning you have the lowest satisfaction and 10 meaning you are perfectly satisfied. Let's call this your "life list." This is a satisfaction survey, meaning how satisfied you are with this area of your life. If you lack an intimate partner, but are satisfied without one at the time, you would score that higher than if you are dissatisfied with your intimate relationship, or do not have one but want one.

Career /profession

Family / parenting

Personal development

Spiritual awareness

Fun & enjoyment

Social relationships

Intimate relationships

Health / aging

Personal finances

High numbers are not your first goal. Your first goal is balance. You won't be able to cope well until you work toward balance. So, if you have eights or nines in one area and twos and threes in another area, you can raise your overall life satisfaction rate by addressing the areas with the lowest number(s) first.

Bear in mind that not all these areas are created equal to each person. If something feels very important to you, then that's your priority area on which to focus.

Normally, in a non-emergent environment, I walk clients through a path of developing a comprehensive plan for setting a goal, creating a plan, taking the steps to get there and holding yourself accountable; however, this survival guide has a different purpose. The purpose of this survival guide is to identify where you most need social interaction to feel recharged, and how you can create the fulfillment you need in this unusual situation.

As an extrovert in isolation, you're starving for social interaction. This brief exercise will tell you where to focus your energy.

LESSON FOUR

Virtual Fulfillment

Is virtual fulfillment for avatars or people?

Virtual fulfillment can be more relevant to humans than to the cartoon characters we more often associate with video games. To examine the role of virtual fulfillment, let's compare two clients: Gina and Trevor.

Gina is both a client and a long-time friend. She sent me a note on Facebook Messenger. It started this way: *"I don't feel like myself with all this virus news going around. It's all anyone ever talks about. I'm ready to be done with it and get back to the gym already. How are you?"*

Since I've known Gina for more than a decade, I knew this was not small talk. This was her cry for help.

Several years ago, when Gina's twins went away to college, she found herself letting her physical health go. For years, she was active in the local high school's parent teacher association. Her husband recommended she take up tennis from her college days. She loved playing tennis with friends until she tore her ACL. After her surgery, she enrolled in Pilates classes to strengthen her knee.

Not only did she strengthen her knee, she made wonderful new friends. In fact, her Pilates classes became her social gathering spot, until gyms in her state were closed due to COVID-19. When that happened, her reason for starting her day went away.

A different client of mine, Trevor, works in sales. He posts on social media regularly for his job. He posts a variety of content to remain top of mind when his prospective customers are ready to buy. He shared that lately, his post traffic is noticeably down.

"I don't want to start posting outrageous things just to get reactions," he said. *"This makes me feel desperate."*

I trolled his Facebook to see how far his posts had diminished in responses, and to be honest, it was minor. I sent back a question: *"Trevor, are you feeling desperate that your traffic is down or are you feeling desperate because you miss your connection to your community?"*

What do Gina and Trevor have in common?

1. They are both extroverts.
2. They are both missing a social connection to their community.
3. They both have extra time on their hands. Time that used to be devoted to filling their energy reserve.

Do you understand what Gina and Trevor are experiencing?

ACTIVITY:

Returning to your "life list," here are examples that a struggling extrovert could do within the isolation confines of COVID-19 to increase their social interaction in any given area.

Career /profession: Hold a contest with your peers: First person to list 3 books with the same "industry specific" word wins. Decide on the word or phrase together and then hit go! Make a list of five things you've always wanted to explore with regard to your career. Now pick one!

Family / parenting: Create a project with your kids, like painting rocks and delivering them to your neighbors with a note that says: *Our world may be social distancing but we're only a few houses away if you need anything.* Post a photo on social media to give others great ideas and to receive feedback from your friends and followers.

Personal development: Find or write positive affirmations and mail them to friends. In addition to making their day when they open their mail, most will reach out to you with a message that will remind you of the difference you make in their lives. Ever wanted to write your life's story, or a novel? Why not give it a shot now?

Spiritual awareness: Pray. Meditate. Participate in a Facebook Live church service online where you can exchange comments with people you know or those hosting the service. Read the Bible. Research world religions. Dive deeper into your faith, or if faith is not important to you, create peace between your energy and the energy around you.

Fun & enjoyment: Find a buddy (or several buddies) with a similar interest. Share photos via text or social media. Exchange videos with friends on Marco Polo. Share your passion and progress. Start a vegetable garden (hardware and garden shops are considered essential in most states). Paint anything: a room, a canvas, rocks, an old table, etc. Try a new recipe and post video clips online. Dye your hair a fun color. Download a new song and groove to it. Name something you've always wanted to try and the try it! Discover something that makes your heart sing.

Social relationships: Set up a virtual "coffee with friends" on Zoom, Google Meets, or a conference line for 30 minutes where you all catch up on non-COVID-19 life events. Invite tons of people. Find ways to integrate sharing and socialization into each area of your life. For an extrovert, sharing is a key piece to replenishing your energy and joy so you can continue to be generous in all you do. (A lot of people have grown tired of video chats. Consider doing something fun to shake it up, like everyone wears the same color shirt or creates a back drop with a similar theme.)

Intimate relationships: If you have an intimate relationship, enjoy each other's company. If you don't have one but want one, meet someone through an online community. Just be safe.

Health & aging: If you're missing your workout companions, why not grab a pair of ear buds and your phone and connect to someone via your phone while you walk, run or hike, as if they were beside you? They can be across town or across the country, but your workout will go faster if you talk to someone while you walk.

Personal finances: Finally write that budget you've been putting off. If you have some extra money, use it to help someone out. If you need resources, ask your circle for help. We all need help sometimes, and most people love to help when we can. Be real and watch the magic and generosity begin to flow.

One positive thing COVID-19 has created through all

this isolation is a chance to try new things and find out what you actually enjoy and what you only thought you'd enjoy. Perhaps you've considered knitting, sewing, gardening, or something else. For non-essential workers who are following a stay-at-home order, you have been given time with your household, time you may never have again to pursue projects, hobbies, and relationships. COVID-19 will pass, but the way you invest this time will last.

LESSON FIVE

Prioritizing Self-Care

Be kind to your future self.

There's a reason that every time you get on an airplane, the pre-flight demonstration includes a piece about securing your own mask in an emergency before you help the person next to you. If you do not prioritize self-care, you cannot take care of those around you. If you take care of others but neglect yourself, at some point, you will pay a price. So be kind to your future self by taking care of yourself so you can take care of others.

For parents, it's natural for your first concern to be for your children. But how many of us prioritize the care of others before we check in with ourselves to ensure we're getting our needs met? If you're an extrovert who's struggling, you need better self-care. The fact that you're reading this survival guide indicates you're aware that you need or want to evaluate your priorities.

- What makes you feel cared for?
- Do you feel pretty or pulled together?
- Are you staying hydrated and well nourished?

- Are you moving throughout your day and getting exercise?
- Specifically, are you investing your time in being your best self?

During this time of stay-at-home orders, quarantine, self-isolation, or whatever you choose to call it, extroverts especially have reported losing a desire to invest in how they look and feel.

Several have reiterated the same message, that without an in-person social network to show up for, and without the services they use to maintain their image (hair and nail salons, waxing studios, tattoo shops all closed during the shut-down), they've lost their desire to even shower and get dressed some days.

When asked if they only dress up for other people, the answer was surprisingly no. Most said some variation of this: *getting ready, showing up and interacting with others is all part of a socializing process.* When you remove the socializing portion, the other pieces do not feel as relevant. **In other words, extroverts are not getting ready for other people; they are getting ready for the entire experience of bringing their best self to the social process.**

For many extroverts, self-care includes the services and the relationships with the people who help them look and feel their best. Their stylist, manicurist, massage therapist are part of this complex network.

ACTIVITY:

Self-care for an extrovert looks different than general self-care. General self-care includes practices that support your physical, emotional, and spiritual well-being. Extroverts need general self-care with a sociability factor added. **How can you incorporate small changes to feel a big difference?**

- What can you find or create that will bring you joy and allow you to connect to others?
- Is it a Zoom meeting with 10 other people gesturing and interrupting each other with exciting news to share?
- Do you have a favorite recipe that you could email or text a photo of to someone special?
- Have you found a new hair or health product that you could buy for yourself and send to a friend? If you can't afford that, perhaps you could send a link to a product to someone and let them know you were thinking of them.
- What about sending a personal note or a card through the mail or postal service?

While social media can be useful during normal times or to share photos of special outings or occasions, social media may not create the level of connectedness that feeds an extrovert's soul during social isolation. A post on social media is more like an advertisement than a connection. Whether you get twenty likes or two hundred, it's only going to provide so much connectivity. **For genuine connectivity, reach out with an individual message to a specific person.**

You have a much higher chance of making a genuine connection that way – a connection that will refill your bright, beautiful, extroverted energy.

LESSON SIX

Go Ahead: Ask for a Hug

Elbow bumps. Side hugs. Air hugs! We all need them!

A well-known community volunteer in Central Washington posted a question on social media when COVID-19 isolation commenced: Would it be wrong for me to ask for a hug?

She wasn't asking for a literal hug; she was reaching out to let her friends know she missed them. More than a hundred of her friends and followers responded with virtual hugs and messages about how much she meant to them. I happened to have a greeting card on hand with a porcupine on the cover, paired with a similar question. I mailed it to brighten her day. She loved the sentiment!

While social distancing in response to COVID-19 prevented friends from physically driving to her house and giving her a physical hug, the tremendous response she received from caring friends and acquaintances recharged her need for connectedness.

Ask for whatever you need to feel connected. Your survival depends on it.

After having so many extroverts reach out to me, I decided to reach out to some of those extroverts in my network who hadn't raised their hands to say hello. I could feel the anguish when I received messages back that included:

"Well, you know I'm a hugger. So, I'm struggling right now."

"I'm working from home. I'm thankful to have an income, but I miss working with people."

"Learning my job is not considered essential killed me. I'd rather be in danger of coming into contact with the virus than be told I'm not essential."

"When I talk to people, I touch them. I squeeze their hand or tap their shoulder. It's really hard to have to stay six feet away from everyone. I feel so disconnected."

"I hate social distancing. A friend of mine offered to have lunch together and sit six feet away. That's like being served a glass of water in front of me and my favorite pasta that I could smell but not taste."

"I talk to people and I touch them. I'm not allowed to do that anymore. I feel shut down."

Each of these statements came from people who clearly refill their energy by sharing a close space with other people.

ACTIVITY:

Have you ever heard of reiki? It's a therapeutic practice whereby the practitioner uses energy and heat to connect with a client instead of using tissue manipulation or massage to impart help or healing. Some people feel tingling or heat.

If you want to experience the exchange of energy and heat, there's an experiment you can try.

Place your hands together, palms facing and then pull them apart one-half inch. Your palms should be facing each other, one-fourth to one-half inch apart.

- Now close your eyes. Do you feel heat between your hands?
- Do you feel energy?

This mirrors the sensation your physical body is receiving when someone casually leans in to greet you or bid farewell with a hug. An actual embrace is the action or reason we use in a polite society for leaning in, but the part that refills an extrovert is the exchange of heat and energy that takes place when two people are one-fourth to one-half inch apart. This is sometimes called "clean touch." It's a non-intimate connection to another person.

Let's try that again.

- Place your palms facing, one-fourth to one-half inch apart and close your eyes.
- Connect with the heat and energy exchange.

If you are an extrovert, close your eyes (this may seem uncomfortable at first, but stay with me and try it for one whole minute), and imagine you are surrounded by friends and strangers. It may help if you turn on music you would enjoy at a party. Do this near a wall and move to the music, eyes closed, hands with palms facing remaining in position to experience a heat exchange, and occasionally bump into the wall with a hip or arm.

Essentially, you are creating an energy exchange in

a pseudo environment that you are intentionally tricking your mind to accept as a social gathering. Obviously, you know the difference, but it is an internal suspension of disbelief that your mind is allowing your body to accept. It's as if your mind is telling your body, "Okay, I guess I'll play along."

If it helps to use a blindfold to prevent yourself from opening your eyes while you are recharging, do that. This exercise is exclusively for you, and in whatever way it best supports you, that's what you should do.

For those of you prone to over-thinking, this exercise is like using an extract to flavor a dish rather than a real ingredient. *It's not the same as a genuine social opportunity. But if you allow your mind to trick your body, you can receive benefit, especially if you allow your mind to imagine a social scenario.*

If you get asked by someone, for instance, one of your introverted friends, if they can use the opposite strategy, the answer is yes. Tell them to merely find a way to step away from a crowd, put the palms together facing, a half-inch apart, and take deep breaths imagining the feelings of safety and time apart to heal and rejuvenate. Again, this is not the same as actually recharging alone, but lets them know that if their mind and body work together, they too can receive some benefit to recharge from this exercise practice.

The most important lesson is to ask for what you need, whether that is social interaction or extra social space. And then honor the unlikely ways in which your request may be granted.

LESSON SEVEN

Create a Game (Plan)

Join a community! Or create one.

Community means different things. It can be a physical community, a community with shared ideology or even a virtual community, as long as it provides a sense of connectedness.

Every community creates their own games, events, traditions, and missions that keep it connected. From hospital guilds to book clubs, faith groups and gatherings of every kind. In virtual gaming and entertainment communities like Twitch and Mixer, there are producers and gamers who stay live for twelve hours or more straight. What gives these gaming producers energy is their connection to their fans, followers, and community.

Today, in this period of quarantine, people who prefer in-person and social communities are finding themselves lost in isolation. But it doesn't have to be this way. As the days turn into weeks, exciting things are happening. Ashes are bubbling up into creativity. People are finding wonderful ways to express and engage in community, even during social distancing.

From drive-by car parades to celebrate birthdays and welcome cancer patients' home from the hospital, to neighborhood dance-offs and balcony sing-a-longs, there are so many creative ways to come together and still practice social distancing.

Families are assembling puzzles together, cooking dinner at home and talking, with phones and digital devices in another room. Kids are painting rocks and riding bikes. Families are throwing pajama parties and when the weather gets warmer, many will be planting vegetable gardens. In many ways, it's reminiscent of life in suburban America in the 1980s.

If you're more of a digital person, download the Houseparty App and play trivia games with up to eight people at a time. Everyone can be physically isolated and still feel socially connected to others who are logged in. The parameters around technology make it functional to the average person now.

A favorite among youth is an App called Among Us. Think of it as a modern-day murder mystery, without the scary parts for kids. Four to ten people can play, and if you want to keep kids safe, just make sure you only include people who are sharing your wifi. Of course there are in-app purchases, that you can disable. The interactions come via text, so turn the settings to private to keep strangers from accessing little ones. This is fun for kids (and adults) of all ages.

Marco. Polo. Many years ago, this was an echo game. One kid would yell Marco, and another would follow-up with Polo. Although the Marco Polo app came out six years ago, it has caught on like TikTok during COVID-19. This is an app you'll want to use and feel good about your kids using. It's not about likes or followers. It's a video messaging and hosting service for cell phones. And it's free, although it includes in-app purchases of which you'll want to be mindful. They have now moved to a rather well-marketed paid version, so be careful if that's not the direction you want to go.

For work and personal communication there are great options: Facebook Live, SLACK, Microsoft Teams, Zoom, Google Hangouts, WhatsApp, and so many more. Many artists and teachers are utilizing Facebook Live to host cooking demonstrations, painting lessons, yoga and exercises that followers can do from their living rooms.

If you want to see some of the creative ways real people are reaching out to connect while they stay home, stay safe and maintain a distance from others, *join our public Facebook group: Social Distancing An Extrovert's Survival Guide.* I'm amazed daily by the awesome ways people are connecting safely.

The next activity starts in this chapter and concludes in the next chapter.

ACTIVITY (PART 1):

Create three lists.

The first list includes your inner circle. Try to include at least two people who do not live with you.

The second list is your outer circle or social list. It can include up to eight friends or people who you normally look forward to seeing at least weekly. This might include fellow parents you see when you drop your kids off at school, a local church group, a favorite co-worker, or someone you volunteer alongside at a local nonprofit. This is someone you normally see and want to continue to interact with during social distancing.

The third list is your community circle, made up of the people who help frame your normal world. Communities can be physical or virtual, but they must be regular parts of your energy source. This might be your manicurist or other self-care specialist. It could include your neighbors, your regular barista, your secretary. It might include people who you regularly run into without even trying. It could be industry colleagues who interact with you and inspire you to learn and grow.

You have your three lists. (By the way, it's totally cool to expand them later.) Next, you're going to create a plan to keep these people in your life.

These familiar faces and people you listed are collectively the folks who refill your energy. You are not going to see all these people while you are social distancing, especially if you (and they) are following stay-at-home government orders. But you will feel empowered, when you create a plan to connect with some of the people who brighten your world.

Next take all three lists and highlight or star two or more people from each list to connect with this week. That's all you need to do for this activity. Make your lists and pick two from each list. This activity is going to continue into the next lesson.

We all know that even the worst storms and circumstances can bring gifts and teach us lessons. Extroverts naturally feel connected to others, recharging in groups both small and large. They feel connected to others, drawing energy from and giving back new energy to their communities. During this period of social distancing, the connections that normally develop naturally are going to take more effort. You can do it! This is a challenge you'll enjoy and that will move your mind from panic to peace.

The COVID-19 virus is without a doubt a catastrophic agent of harm. COVID-19 has set in motion waves of death, isolation, and quarantine. And yet through its pain, it is also bringing unification. People who once shared nothing in common, are now looking out for each other.

Healthcare providers show up to provide care, risking themselves and their own families. Brave employees in grocery stores, banks, pharmacies, restaurants, and other essential businesses are working to keep communities functioning; those with jobs are working to keep the vulnerable safe and small businesses open. Countries are working together to join hands and help around the world. We are all learning to treat each other with kindness, care, and respect.

LESSON EIGHT

Live with a Spirit of Celebration

It's time to get your party started.

The leading physicians and top advisors cannot predict how long COVID-19 will shutter country borders and continue to plead with people to maintain physical distancing. We are now seeing a second global wave that's producing some concerning numbers when it comes to transmission and death. What is certain is that social distancing does not need to mean social disconnectedness.

Society is healthier and people feel happier when we continue to celebrate our special events and achievements, even though those celebrations are going to look different than they did pre-COVID-19.

We see videos of people in towns in Italy singing opera from their balconies. Drive-by birthday caravans have replaced close gatherings that simply are not safe right now.

There are legitimate disappointments for youth missing proms, graduations, benchmark birthdays, and more. People who have planned weddings, especially destination weddings, where a dozen friends have purchased airline tickets or pre-bought travel packages, are concerned about everything from investments to whether their guests will have paid time off (PTO) at work, especially if they have spent it down with COVID-19.

As an extrovert, you are a doer. You get things done! Whatever happens, do not allow yourself to worry about things outside of your control, because that is going to limit your ability to get things done.

A client of mine lives in Washington state and her family lives across the country. Her parents are aging, and she expressed "worry" about possibly needing to fly back east. What if the flights were full? And what if...? She had a list of things that might not work out, and they all concerned her.

We stopped. I asked her to divide her situation (and every situation) into two parts: what we know and what we don't yet know. In my client's case, her two options looked like this:

1. She <u>was not called</u> to leave her home in Washington to care for her parents across the U.S.

2. She <u>was called</u> to leave her home in Washington to care for her parents across the U.S.

Worry creates something we call catabolic energy, which tears away at our well being.

Worry depletes our resources to accomplish productivity. When we do not guard our minds, worry moves in like smoke under a door in a house fire. It overtakes us, and this can disorient us.

In coaching, we make choices that move us into

anabolic energy. **Anabolic energy builds us up.** Anabolic energy is what **drives extroverts to go, do, be, share, help, give, love and lead projects, teams and revolutions that change our world.** My client is a quiet extrovert. She impacts her community. But like so many, she was depleted; worry had nearly snuffed out her helpful anabolic fire keeping her toasty warm and comfortable, and created smoke, taking over her mind and depleting her energy.

My client took a single piece of paper and drew a line down the middle. On the left she wrote "Not called to leave Washington" and on the right side she wrote "Called to leave Washington."

I asked her to brainstorm all the things she could do to support her parents from across the US if they did not get sick and she was not called to leave her home to help them. She listed things like: Send a homemade care package; order necessities to be delivered, send cards, call, video conferencing, and pray for their health, safety, and protection. *These are all productive actions doers can take instead of worrying.*

Next, I asked her to brainstorm the actions she could take if she received word her parents were diagnosed with COVID-19, an they needed her help. The unknown aspect of this diagnosis triggered her to express worry. She stated she didn't even know if the airports would be open or how she would get back if the situation deteriorated. *"There are so many unknowns,"* she expressed.

So how do we plan in the face of the unknown?

We don't plan the unknown. We only plan what we know.

We **plan the steps we will take** not knowing what future options will present. For my client this meant **her**

action item was simply to wait and only *list the transportation options available at the time she was needed to travel to see her family (not now).*

"*I can't plan anything now. What if I need to leave quickly and I forget an option?*" she asked. "What if I get called to go and need to leave immediately?" she asked.

"Very well. Let's say you received a call that you were needed to help your parents. What would you do first?" I questioned.

"I'd call an airline, of course. Unless airports are shut down. Do you think I need a list?" she asked.

Fear can drive anxiety, especially in a pandemic or situation that feels overwhelming and completely outside of our control. My client didn't need to make a list because she already had a plan; however, if she was making a list, I recommended she 1) wait to make the list until she received the call to go help her parents, and 2) that she included all of the options available at that time, even those she knew she didn't want.

- An airplane
- A bus
- A train
- A car

She stated she had zero desire to ride a bus across the United States, and in fact, wouldn't consider it.

Why would anyone consider adding an "option" they are 100% not willing to do to?

It's actually beneficial to add options you're not willing to consider to your list. Listing an option does not mean you'll change your mind. But it increases your number of choices. More choices equate to increased satisfaction with whatever path you end up choosing. So, go ahead and add it, to remind yourself that you have choices. **If you're going to have the same outcome, wouldn't you rather feel better about your outcome?**

Worry is never your friend. Worry achieves nothing positive and includes no action item other than eating up your mind and digestive system.

Replacing worry by telling yourself that it's okay or it doesn't matter is even worse. That's lying to yourself, because it does matter. And you know it.

ACTIVITY (PART 2):

Now is the time to get creative. Sit down with a blank piece of paper and get creative. List all the ways you can celebrate within this new normal. Google "social distancing celebrations" to see what others are doing. There are great ideas out there. People are resilient. **YOU are resilient. You can do this.**

If you're an extrovert, list-making may not be your favorite activity. But this one's important. Write down things you would enjoy doing to connect with others. In this case, only add activities you would enjoy, and skip "good ideas" that do not feed your soul or bring you joy.

Now, take out your three lists from the last lesson: your inner circle, outer circle, and community circle.

Look at the names you highlighted. Beside each of those names match up an activity or celebration you can use to connect with your village, circle, or tribe.

The importance of the activity is that **as an extrovert you lead the charge to take back your schedule, routine, and life.** If you need additional ideas, check out the list that's included in the next lesson.

45

LESSON NINE

Making the Best Choice

You get to choose. Really. You get to choose!

It's hard to think about a second round of COVID-19 while some states and counties never fully reopened from round one. Yet here we are at the crossroads of flu season and round two of COVID-19 as snow has already started falling in the Northern Hemisphere.

If you're exhausted, you're not alone. More than half a year of our normal way of life being shut down has taken a toll on everyone physically, emotionally, mentally, financially, and in our relationships.

The pandemic has taken its toll on both personal relationships and communities. It has pushed people to a point where differences have been magnified by pain and outrage has poured out. Opinions about in-school versus virtual learning, politics, and orders to wear masks divide us when in reality, our shared common enemy is actually a virus. It's ugly, exhausting and for the most part, unproductive.

There are tools to separate yourself from the drama and start to feel productive in the next 20 minutes.

ACTIVITY:

In 10 words, name one thing that makes you feel powerless or that causes your struggle.

(Ex: Balancing work with educating my children.)

You can do this same exercise with 15 different stressors. Just make sure you fully tackle one at a time before moving forward to the next. Part of what drives stress (negative catabolic energy) in our bodies and minds, is when everything we're facing gets tangled up together like a group of fine chains that wrap around each other. Our first step is to untangle the chains.

Instead of brainstorming everything that's triggering you right now, write down three things, on three separate pieces of paper that you can tackle in the next 30 days.) Keep another notepad or piece of paper nearby. If something else pops into your mind to distract you, write it down on the fourth sheet to come back to later.

1. Choose one concern that you have written down in 10 words or fewer.

2. List all your options for addressing your concern, in no particular order.

(Example. If you have selected schooling your children, your options may include in-person learning at a location. Many private schools that do not receive federal funds are open in places where public schools are providing virtual learning.)

3. Research what is feasible for you.

This may involve making some calls. An informed decision is always a better decision.

4. Considering everything you have learned, make the decision that is right for you by considering these four elements: Is there opportunity? Is it feasible? Is it compatible? Is it the most workable of your options?

Back to our example: Balancing work with educating my children.

- PATH 1: In-person learning.
    - Is there an option for in-person learning? Is space available?
    - If no, move to path 2.
    - If yes, is it feasible? Can I afford it or are there scholarships?
    - Is the transportation manageable?
    - Is this the best option for balancing all my commitments?
- PATH 2: Virtual learning.
    - What are the necessary tools to learn?
    - How do I access them?
    - Can I balance helping my child and completing my work?

    If yes, what arrangements can provide the best environment?

    If no, can I pod-share or school-pool with other parents to each take four other kids one day a week, allowing for a 10-hour workday four days a week?

    Are there other creative ways to create more balance?

> - Is this the best option for balancing all my commitments?

No one is saying this is your idea, or you chose this. But you can choose elements of it. You get to choose how you show up. Creating a plan like this does not infer that you agree with the decisions that have been made outside of your control. But instead of getting angry, you can get a head start on creating balance and productivity. Once you understand your options, you can regain control of your life by putting yourself back in the driver's seat.

This doesn't take away your voice. It simply gives you back your sense of empowerment.

There are circumstances outside of our control. Many families life with physical, mental or emotional challenges that cannot be wished away. It's important to remember this when thinking about someone who may need a little extra grace. Sometimes that's a neighbor or a friend, and sometimes, it's us! We all need grace.

Homeschooling has emerged as an exceptionally difficult challenge for most families, include those where one parent or guardian is a trained educator.

A mom in Colorado shared her story on national news about educating and caring for her two sons, both with significant special needs. At one point, she broke down talking to the reporter. Prior to COVID-19, both of her sons had been assigned one-on-one nurses in their local public school. Because of the virus, not only were her beautiful boys home with her all day, it was not deemed safe for the local school district to provide respite care.

Whitney Stohr-Hendrickson, a child advocate attorney and mother of a child with special needs in Lynnwood, Washington, frames the importance of community for families managing a special needs component in COVID-19.

"COVID-19 has been especially challenging for a lot of families with school age children. Depending on the disability, the kids may qualify in their IEPs for one-on-one learning aids," Stohr-Hendrickson said. "Parents of kids with autism are struggling because these children need routine to thrive and the routines they had established in school were ripped away virtually overnight." She says virtual schooling is especially difficult for kids with disabilities who rely on routines.

What can families do to make the most of this time? "It's important to find the good. Even though this is a scary, stressful time, there is a lot of good around us right now," Stohr-Hendrickson said. She says that now is the time to invest in family relationships, when possible, and establish new traditions. "Find new favorite activities as a family. Consider the positive things we can take forward with us after this is over. For our family, this includes new skills, cooking together, gardening, painting and creating."

What can friends, neighbors and others do to support parents of children with special needs? Stohr says it's the little things that make a big difference:

1. Offer to help with small tasks or errands that need to be checked off the to-do list.
2. Reach out and set up a Zoom play date for kids.
3. Drop off a meal, or a bottle of wine or seltzer with an encouraging note.
4. Share virtual parent support groups. If you find

them helpful, someone else may also.

Above all, just let people know you care. Sometimes the best gift is the reminder that there is a community or tribe out there willing to share the path. Physical distancing does not need to equal social isolation. Physical distancing is inconvenient. Social isolation kills the spirit. You get to choose how you frame and accept the current reality. Remember, it's not forever, just for now.

LESSON TEN

*Living in Today While
Planning for Tomorrow*

Think of it as packing for a vacation or planning for a very long snow day.

Hoarding leads to clutter and clutter can have an oppressive impact on your life. Planning ahead by purchasing a responsible number of necessary items can prevent the stress and concern of struggling to find high demand items like toilet paper and disposable cleaning wipes.

Many people spent the first half of 2020 searching for basic household items that were unavailable in local stores. One way to make sure this doesn't happen to you is to spend one week making a list of items you can't live without for four to six weeks. It makes sense to stock up on items you'll need to feel safe and comfortable should the world return to isolation for any period of time.

To get the low down on what many working parents are thinking, facing and doing, I invited nurse and mother, Laura Hefner, RN, to share her best advice on the public Facebook group, Social Distancing, An Extrovert's Survival Guide. She shared five of her top considerations.

1. You can never have enough art supplies! It saves the sanity as a parent to hand over a new box of crayons/markers/coloring book/glue sticks/ googly eyes to my children ages four and seven to have a second of calm while I get my caffeine and pry open my eyes.

2. The emotional meltdowns just happen, and you never know which one is going to blow next. At our house, the adults have had more meltdowns than the kids, but we are working on our apologies and giving each other grace.

3. Mental health is so very important, now more that ever when we find so much time without the distractions to keep the depression in check. As a nurse, I see this more than you can possibly imagine. The amount of suicides attempts, both successful and non successful, are impacting more lives than COVID 19. Let that sink in. So, get outside in the sun. Soak up the vitamin D, with the appropriate sunscreen of course. Work out or get active doing something strenuous. Write cards and letters to stay connected. Call your friends and talk.

4. Staying physically healthy, and keep washing your hands, even if it makes them feel dry. Washing your hands is truly the No. 1 way to limit the spread of germs. Also, eating well and getting good sleep are super important. It's hard when one day morphs into the next. If you wear yourself out or deprive your body of what it needs to survive, you will not make it through this pandemic as well. Bandages, Tylenol, ice packs, and

hydrogen peroxide will serve you well in keeping most minor things controlled at home.

5. If you live in a town with one hospital, investigate airlift transportation insurance. One trip can cost ten times the cost of insurance for a whole. When a hospital hits capacity, patients requiring hospitalization may be reassigned to a nearby city or state. One hospital may not be enough in a pandemic.

There are some awesome craft recipes online that can keep little hands occupied for hours. YouTube and Pinterest can be great resources for fresh ideas. If you're not a social media savvy person, I've invited blogger Melea June Brown, an essential oil expert with Oil and Shine, to share her favorite dough for kids below. She adds essential oils to either give kids energy (peppermint) or calm them before bed (lavender). Brown says one of her favorite combinations includes orange, cinnamon and nutmeg, as it "smells like fall."

For home crafters, Melea sent over her tried and true recipe for family fun, with permission to share it. Thanks, Melea!

Oil and Shine Kids' Dough Non-Edible Recipe*

Kids love to play and create. This version was adapted to feel great, smell great and offer all around fun. Working with our hands can be a great stress reliever at any age. Whether you're making this for little ones or teens, this non-edible kids dough is a great idea for kids and kids-at-heart.

To ensure you have all the ingredients, check your cupboards and stock up on anything you may need. If you're into healthy activities, you may appreciate this healthy "play" recipe that gives kids something to build with their hands and minds.

INGREDIENTS:

1 cup of flour (if you have an allergy, use a 1-to-1 replacement flour)

2 tsp cream of tarter

1/2 cup salt

1 tbsp cooking oil

1 cup water

6-8 drops of essential oil

*To make it festive add 2-3 drops of food coloring.

INSTRUCTIONS:

1. In a large bowl, combine all of your dry ingredients and mix well.

2. Add the cooking oil and water to a large pot and mix together.

3. Add the dry ingredients (and optional food coloring) to your pot and mix well.

4. Cook over low to medium heat until the dough starts to form and becomes dry.

5. When it starts to form a ball together and looks fully cooked, take off of heat. Let the dough cool.

6. Once cool, knead in 6-8 drops of essential oil. For calming effects use lavender. Peppermint would be a fun one too that is good for the senses. Have fun experimenting. I recommend high quality therapeutic oils, like Young Liv-

ing essential oils.

*Shared with permission.

LESSON ELEVEN

Think of this as activity **BINGO. How many boxes can you check?**

If you have kids or remember being one, you know the phrase: "When are we gonna get there?" Extroverts were the first to report feeling lost and lonely because of social distancing. The longer people are separated from friends and family through social distancing, the more people of all personality types are appreciating simple activities like hugs, happy hours, and social gatherings.

When COVID-19 initially hit, people experienced withdrawal from common occurrences once taken for granted: open restaurants and busy malls, hot yoga and fitness classes, sporting events, science fairs, state fairs, and church services. In the United States, well-stocked grocery stores and catching up with friends at community fundraisers were an assumed normal.

Suddenly, we missed the only life we had ever known. We missed our people.

In the spring of 2020, my personal group of six

friends jumped on Marco Polo at least weekly, sometimes more, to update each other on everything from facial peels, to recipes, and project updates. I found out my friend Pam loves to mow her lawn and my friend Kyleen, a teacher, was guiding 142 students through schooling at home. Both impressed me!

For those clients (or friends asking for coaching) who were climbing the walls, and feeling a need to break out of their own homes, we brainstormed things folks could do to connect outside of virtual calls and games. (Who doesn't have a love-hate relationship with Zoom and Teams at this point?)

I also reached out to the members of the Facebook group: Social Distancing, An Extrovert's Survival Guide. (Come join us.) Here's a month's worth of creative ideas.

- **Spring-Sing-Along**: A high school choir teacher invited her students to join her in standing six plus feet apart and singing numbers from the musical they never got to perform to random neighbors.
- **Coffee Delivery**: One woman's husband wanted to go for a drive. She missed her colleagues and they both missed their favorite coffee. They ordered six coffees through the drive-up. One for each of them and four additional drinks for her colleagues. They drove around to their homes, dropping off coffee. Waves and hellos from the curb replaced Zoom squares on the laptop.
- **Garden Clean-up**: Instead of gathering in enclosed greenhouses, a gardening club in Oregon mapped out a handful of shut-ins and showed up in pairs to remove leftover leaves and plant spring flowers.

- **Dude's Nightcap**: One man invited three of his neighbors to his backyard one night after work, all sitting at a distance, sharing laughs and double shots of their favorite scotch. Just four guys kicking back to talk about life or nothing at all can really raise the spirits.
- **Tailgating Light**: Six friends with pick-up trucks met in a parking lot, tailgates down. They backed their trucks together to create a hexagon, each truck 10 feet apart to accommodate social distancing for anyone moving around. Each brought their own food and shared conversation, in person.
- **Break a Leg**: A theatre group couldn't perform live in front of an audience. Instead, they adapted their choreography to incorporate social distancing, recorded songs and dances and performed for a camera to upload to YouTube. Instead of a packed theatre, their audience was at home.
- **Baked with Love**: Cookies for everyone. Kaitlin and her mom are sharing joy to their friends and family by dropping off plates of freshly baked cookies right to their front door. What an awesome way to share a snack with those you appreciate.
- **Yoga in the Park**: A yoga instructor in California leads small groups of four people through semi-private non-assisted outdoor yoga sessions in a local park. Each participant is at least 20 feet apart and must bring their own mat, towel, and any accessories.
- **Sisterhood of the Traveling Sign**: No one knows who started this, but someone made a portable

lawn sign that says: "Attention: A Super Awesome Person Lives Here. Honk If You Can Read This." A weathered piece of paper with the directions is hung on the front door of the yard where the sign is placed. It says: "Share the joy. After 48 hours, please relocate this sign to someone else's yard to brighten their day, and tape this note to their door."

- **Messages in Chalk**: "Miss your face! (heart)" One lady reported walking out her front door one morning to colored chalk pictures and messages on her sidewalk from her neighbor. It made her feel so good that she enlisted the help of her kids and they walked around their neighborhood drawing rainbows, hearts and sunshine alongside positive messages like, "Good morning, beautiful," and "Summer is coming."

- **Let Them Eat Cake**: One lady's voice lit up when she talked about ordering a special cake at her favorite bakery. The owner was happy to see her, which made her feel like her business mattered. She tipped well to show her appreciation for the service and to help local venues allowed to stay open. When you frequent the same small businesses, they'll get to know you and look forward to your return.

- **Neighborly Love**: When the Happicks found out they were having a boy, they announced it on Facebook but were sad they couldn't have a party or share the news with neighbors. They ordered a delivery of blue Mylar balloons and tied them to their mailbox. A few days later, their neighbors hung a banner on their house that said: Congratulations on your baby boy!

- **Neighborhood Bingo**: A cul-de-sac in Illinois plays neighborhood BINGO on Saturdays. Bingo cards are distributed Saturday mornings, and each family sets up chairs in their own driveway; someone calls the numbers. Participating families each donate a high-demand prize: Clorox wipes, snacks and dessert, alcohol and of course toilet paper.
- **Set a Gratitude Goal**: Send cards, leave voicemails, call people out on social media for being awesome, and go out of your way to thank people (especially healthcare workers and essential employees) for their work.
- **Good Morning Sunshine**: Coffee is a morning-starter for a lot of people, but when you're stuck at home, how can you access freshly roasted coffee beans? A nonprofit in Central Washington State, is hosting a fundraiser to support their work in creating a drug free community and providing youth mentoring. They deliver bags of whole or ground coffee throughout the area with community resources to keep youth and families safe.
- **Create a Kindness Project**: Look around. When you see someone in need, find a way to give help, show kindness or help in some way big or small. You can make a meaningful difference and making a difference will make you feel more connected to your community. Free template at www.thekindnessproject.club.
- **Holiday Delivery**: For Easter, a newspaper journalist wanted to show appreciation for all the si-

lent local volunteers she covered for stories while they were helping to pass food out to families. So, she put together baskets to deliver anonymously Easter morning.

- **Drawing a Masterpiece**: An elementary art specialist wanted her students to know how important they are to her, even while apart. On a poster board she wrote in many colors: Hi L&C Students. I miss you! Keep on creating every day! Love your art teacher, Mrs. Boyle. Los extraño machismo.
- **Spring Cleaning**: Many people at home are sorting garages and spare rooms. CenterCal Properties, which owns more than 20 properties in Washington, Oregon, California, Idaho, and Utah, is empowering their local shopping centers to help their local communities. The Valley Mall in Union Gap, Washington teamed up with the county's Office of Emergency Management to host a supplies "drive-up drop-off" area for people with extra non-latex gloves, masks, hand sanitizer, bleach or other needed medical supplies could donate them to the local hospital's healthcare providers.
- **Call-in Congregation**: Reverend Carolyn Williamson from Mt. Hope Baptist Church serves a mostly African American congregation where many are unable to access services online. But they all have radios. Neighborhood churches spread the word that she'd be live on the radio Easter Sunday taking requests. Parishioners gathered around home radios to worship and pray for local families with unspoken prayers.
- **Saturday Morning Cinnamon Rolls**: Fresh, hot,

soft, gooey cinnamon rolls. They're a hit at fund-raisers and as a special treat at home. When Ann's kids beg for cinnamon rolls, she makes a very large batch. She sends out a call for hot rolls and a friendly visit. Saturday mornings, she meets friends at a local spot. Instead of sitting across a table, friends visit across the hood of her car. Her friends leave with hot cinnamon rolls and she covers the cost of her ingredients.

- **Zoom in on a Work of Art**: Sheila Grace, the painting instructor who created the cover of this survival guide, teaches online painting classes while following a statewide stay-at-home order. Through Zoom, painters can all focus the camera on their paintings instead of them, and then turn it around at the end to put a face with their art. She also teaches traditional classes on Facebook Live where she teaches step-by-step and students follow along.

- **A Birthday Toast**: For Whitney's 33rd birthday, her friends bought her a bottle of her favorite wine and a birthday wine glass. They created a beautiful basket and left it outside her door before she woke up. To avoid waking her, instead of ringing her doorbell, they hung signs and good wishes for her to find when she opened her blinds. The signs led her to the basket.

- **Make Mine A Double**: Every Thursday the Shareef and Jones families get together for pizza and game night. After two weeks in quarantine, the Shareefs decided to have game night at home, order a pizza for themselves, and order a second one to send to their friends. The Jones family had the same idea on the same night. Both families ended up with two pizzas. They each got a good laugh and decided going forward to coordinate so pizza and game night could continue.

- **Peanut Butter and Crayons**: The Hershberger family created a care package for grandpa, who had to be isolated for his protection. The package included his favorite peanut butter cookies, hand-drawn pictures and notes from his grandkids, and a framed school picture. Rachel's recipe appears at the end of this chapter.
- **Positive Postal Revolution**: As many households move to home delivery for everything from groceries to supplies and more, postal service workers and other delivery drivers can frequently be seen running to get everything delivered on time and in good condition. Friends Kim and Lisa started a positive postal revolution. Lisa, who refers to herself as a hippie at heart, and Kim, send at least one letter, card, drawing, photo or gift through the mail daily to let people know they're being thought about and to keep jobs for postal workers. Lisa takes it a step further and includes cards or gifts for her mailperson to thank them for their hard work!
- **Book It Forward**: Many people, especially readers, have shelves filled with books they would love to share. To get started, take your stack of books, from two to ten, and put them in a pile to distribute. Then inside add a piece of paper that says, "I enjoyed this book. Hope you will too. When you are finished, pass it on (or another book of your choosing) with this note to someone else. Let's

keep people reading and the joy flowing." It will be interesting to see if another book mysteriously shows up at your door.

- **TikTok Bar Crawl**: For the grownups, pick a few of your friends' favorite beverages (alcohol or virgin), deliver the ingredients (illegal to send alcohol through the mail but you can always drop at a doorstep), and then meet up on social media, Marco Polo or Zoom and share your day over happy hour. It's all about connecting while staying at home if you can.

- **Family Bear Hunts**: Communities across the US are encouraging families to place a stuffed bear in a street-facing window. Then, when families go for walks to get exercise, the kids can go on a bear hunt to make the walk in their neighborhood more fun.

- **Forget-Me-Not**: In the Northern Hemisphere, it's spring and soon to be summer. Send seeds. From flowers to zucchini seeds, seeds are like giving someone a box of harvest in an envelope. Plus, when they bloom or turn into produce, they'll think of you. If you're delivering in person, it might be nice to include a few cups of soil. Kindness brings connection to the giver and receiver.

- **Hands Together**: We've all seen pictures of loved ones, separated by glass, hands pressed together. Try tracing the small hands and adult hands on each side of the glass. When the visitor has returned home, the handprints are left behind as a reminder of time together.

For home chefs out there, Rachel sent over her dad's

favorite peanut butter cookie recipe, along with permission to share it. Thanks, Rachel!

Rachel's Heavenly Peanut Butter Cookies*

INGREDIENTS:

1 and 1/2 cups all purpose flour

1/2 teaspoon baking soda

1/4 teaspoon salt

1/2 cup unsalted butter, softened to room temperature

3/4 cup light brown sugar

1/4 cup granulated sugar

3/4 cup creamy peanut butter

1 large egg room temperature

1 teaspoon vanilla extract

3 tablespoons granulated sugar

INSTRUCTIONS:

Preheat oven to 350°F. Line two large baking sheets with parchment paper or silicone baking mats and set aside.

In a large mixing bowl, whisk together the flour, baking soda, and salt. Set aside.

In the bowl of a stand mixer fitted with the paddle attachment, or in a large mixing bowl using an electric mixer, cream together the butter, brown sugar, and granulated sugar for 1-2 minutes until well combined.

Add in the peanut butter and continue mixing until well combined, stopping to scrape down the sides of the bowl as needed. Mix in the egg and vanilla extract until fully combined. Slowly add in the dry ingredients and mix until just combined.

Place the 3 tablespoons of granulated sugar in a small bowl. Using a two-tablespoon cookie scoop, scoop the dough from the bowl, roll into a ball, and coat in the granulated sugar. Place each ball of cookie dough on the prepared baking sheets, making sure to leave a little room between each one. Gently press down with a fork on the top of each cookie to make a small criss-cross pattern.

Bake at 350°F for 10-12 minutes or until the tops are set. Remove from the oven and allow to cool on the baking sheet for 5-10 minutes, then carefully transfer to a wire rack to finish cooling.

*Published with permission

LESSON TWELVE

A SMART Approach

It all starts with the first step.

Want to achieve your goals? Here's How! Goals can be a tricky subject during COVID. For some people, setting a goal equates to setting themselves up for failure and they just don't want another thing to go wrong. If you're feeling this, you're not alone. We've all been there.

Here's the thing: if you have a dream without a plan, your dream will never be more than a dream. It would be like having a dream to go on vacation but never buying a plane ticket or putting gas in the car. Most people dream about something they would actually like to do.

A dream remains a dream until it's backed up by solid goal setting. What if you could have a dream, set a goal, and be assured you would get there -- with no pressure about changing the arrival date as you continued to make a series of choices along the way? That might be less intimidating.

The truth is, we achieve dreams and goals every day that do not scare us. If you've ever arrived at an appointment on-time, you achieved a goal. What can feel scary is when we want something that's extra important to us, but we either feel unworthy, unlucky or unable to make it happen.

The first thing we're going to do is remove the un. The next thing we're going to do is set a SMART goal.

A SMART goal is specific, measureable, attainable, realistic and timely. Set a goal about something you feel confident you will do. It could be to help your child pass math. It could be to finish a report. It could be to organize a spare bedroom or clean out your garage. Maybe in your quest to save money or eat healthier, your goal is to make dinner at home three nights a week. Whether you like the task or not, set a goal for something you will end up doing, whether you plan for it or not. By doing this, you are teaching your mind that you have the power to win. **You have the power to reach your goal.**

Often in sports, coaches will attempt to schedule easier teams on the front end of the playing season if they can. Why is this? It's to teach the athletes how it feels to win, so they have that taste for victory when the competition gets tougher.

Whether you realize it or not, you win every single day. You get the laundry done and have fresh clothes: that's a win. You eat, cooked at home or to go: that's a win. You make it to appointments on time: another win. If you were to create a checklist of all the things you do, those are all wins.

Now let's talk about what you really want. Specifically, what is something you want? How will you measure it? How can you break it down into steps and pieces and take incremental steps forward? Is your goal attainable? Is it realistic? If your goal is to win the lottery to get out of debt, it's probably not attainable or realistic. If your goal is to get out of debt, you can set up an action plan that is specific, measurable, attainable, realistic, and timely.

Sometimes we want to want something, but we don't want it enough to take the steps necessary to get there. This happens for one of two reasons. Either our timetable is not realistic, or our procrastination or self-sabotage is somehow serving us. If that happens, first, give yourself some grace. Then ask, "How is my procrastination serving me?" Sometimes it's because what we believe we want is really a core value instilled in us by an outside factor? (i.e., *I should want this. I guess I want this. In a perfect world I would want this. My friends or family love me, and they want this for me.*)

Throw out all the "shoulds" from others. What do you want? What are you willing to work to achieve?

Here's the truth: every choice you make serves you. Life coaching can help you ask yourself how your current behaviors are silently serving you.

COVID has turned our world upside-down. It's been catastrophic in so many ways. But it can also be a safe excuse or crutch for avoiding something that's difficult to face. Here's where life coaching and therapy differ. Therapy seeks to solve it. Coaching helps to create awareness, so that when you are ready, you can push through it with a SMART goal.

A few weeks ago, I was talking to Jen Mallinger, a fellow coach in Bothell, Washington, who specializes in home office space design, about what a mess my own living room had become. A portion of space is a mini home office and the rest of the room had become overrun with work papers, Christmas cards and wrap, canned jars, and an eclectic grouping of useful things that had not been put away. It wasn't stuff that needed to be thrown away, or recycled. Some of it was already earmarked as holiday gifts for specific people. But it was a mess.

When my friend and colleague asked how "the mess" was serving me, I was confused. It wasn't serving me. But it was there and although I was bothered by it, I was not bothered enough to change it. Then something happened. She asked me a series of questions I would normally ask my coaching clients (questions I didn't want to ask myself.)

Even with all the tools, sometimes it's helpful to have someone else ask the questions. When she asked me those questions, I had to admit to myself that I was overwhelmed by some life choices I had been avoiding. The mess had nothing to do with the physical stuff, but it was easier for me to blame my internal struggle on the fact that I was overwhelmed by my physical chaos.

When I figured that out, I was finally able to start creating a plan to better manage my time, expectations and my physical space. And I was able to address those things I had been hiding in a corner of my mind. It was uncomfortable and hard. Coaching can be hard. But ignoring the things that bind us prevent us from creating the outcomes we internally need and want to live our best lives.

How do you Get SMART when it comes to making a plan?

Be Specific
"What is it that you want to accomplish, and why?"

"When and where will you achieve this goal, and who will be involved in achieving it?"

"What are the challenges and constraints involved in achieving this goal?"

"What can you offer other people, in order to obtain their assistance towards achieving your goal?"

Measure Your Progress!

"How many/how much do you want to achieve?"

"How will you know if you are on track towards achieving this goal?"

"How will you know when you have achieved this goal (in terms of numbers)?"

Set an Attainable Goal

"Are you comfortable working on this goal right now?" "Why/why not?"

"What are the steps that you need to take in order to achieve your goals?"

"Are you able to grow and expand in order to attain seemingly impossible goals? "

Be Realistic

"What are the factors that may affect the outcome of this goal?"

"How much of this goal is under your direct control?"

"Can you do anything, to bring some of these factors under your control?"

"How will this goal help you to attain happiness or fulfillment?"

"Is this goal aligned with your values, strengths, and needs?"

Set a Timely Pace

"What can be done towards achieving this goal?"

"What can you do in the next 5 days/5 weeks/5 months?"

It all starts with the first step. Once you have a SMART goal, what is the first step you need to take to commence your plan? It could be as simple as making a phone call, researching or making a list of options, separating papers or finishing the dishes. When you eat a meal, you do so one bite at a time. You don't open your mouth, tip back your head and slide everything on your plate in at once. But somehow, when it comes to projects, we get overwhelmed taking things one bite at a time.

Imagine your project is a meal, and start with the first bite. Then take a second and a third. Pace yourself. If you start getting full or overwhelmed, take a breather. But don't go start another meal. You can do this! Of course it's not easy, but it is rewarding when you complete a goal.

LESSON THIRTEEN

What a Great Plan!

Who's starting to feel empowered?

Life may not be normal, but it can still be good. If COVID-19 is still a threat that keeps you from gathering with friends, or gently touching the arm of a stranger when you talk to them, perhaps now you've found new ways to connect. Remember, while it's safer to be physically distant, it's important to maintain emotional connections.

It's normal to feel sad, anxious or a little dark some days. After all, the life you've always known has changed. Many of the routines and activities you once looked to for joy are different. Give yourself 30 minutes or a few hours to mourn the life you knew. Then remind yourself, this is temporary. Look how far you've come over the last twelve lessons.

You're full of great ideas. You've got this! And now you've learned to ask for what you need, from yourself and others. When I lived in Los Angeles, I had a friend who periodically would call me up, invite me to lunch and ask if she could treat me to a nice meal in exchange for me exclusively listening to her externally process all the thoughts in her head.

The first time she said, "I need today to be 100% about me. I'll buy lunch and I need you to just listen and ask questions about me," I thought it was incredibly weird. Then she added, "If you ever just need someone to listen, call me up, treat me to lunch and I will listen to you." Initially, it felt rather transactional, especially since we were friends. (She was a bridesmaid in my wedding.)

Over time, this once peculiar request somehow felt increasingly normal. In fact, it went a step further and made me feel honored. How many times has someone offered, "Call me if you need anything." Maybe you have made that same offer. Do we really mean it? In this arrangement, instead of one person monopolizing the conversation, and the other person feeling ignored, the ground rules were established upfront, and both people contributed to the resolve.

Everyone needs to feel heard, and there's nothing that kills a relationship like one person doing all the talking all the time. That is, unless the ground rules are set up in advance and the active listener has an opportunity to feel needed and appreciated for their skills as an excellent listener. Healthy expectations and good boundaries create the best relationships!

Extroverts love to talk and share. There's no need to feel badly if you're usually the one doing most of the talking. Awareness is the golden gift. Once you acknowledge how much you appreciate the good listeners in your life who help you process what's on your heart, you'll enjoy finding creative ways to thank and reward them for helping to shoulder your load.

Life is a series of puzzle pieces. As difficult as COVID-19 has been on most people, it has provided a grand opportunity to hit the reset button as we all take the time and space to evaluate what it is we need and want. And it's created a beautiful opportunity to start asking for what we want and making time for the people who need what we have to give and give what we need to receive. To get a great fit, the pieces simply need to fit together.

You've got this!! When in doubt, make a plan. You are a doer. It may require more effort for you to feel connected in an environment of social distancing, but if anyone can cut through obstacles, it's you.

FINAL ACTIVITY:

For every challenge, concern, obstacle, barrier, or decision that stands between you and joy, there are always two parts. **Break down your obstacle into what you know and what you don't know.** Only deal with what you know.

- Either I live in the present or I worry about the many possibilities of the future. (The future is unknown.)
- Either I keep my job, or I lose my job.
- Either I don't need to fly across the country, or I do.
- Either we have the resources we need (food, shelter, utilities, transportation) or we don't.
- Either the test is positive or it's not.

Next, stay in the present. It's temping in a crisis, especially a world pandemic, to let your mind wander. Do not let your mind wander. To stay calm, you must stay present. To live in joy, you must stay present. Ask yourself: *What can I do now and what can I set aside until I have more information?*

Make a list of what you can do with the information you have right now. When extroverts stop doing, caring, sharing, and helping, they start worrying and spinning inside. Add to that social distancing and you may start driving yourself or those around you to a place of extreme discomfort. Make a list of things you can do right away to connect to your community.

One of the most amazing survival stories is of a 106-year-old Canadian great grandmother, Bertha Roy, who survived the 1918 Spanish Flu when she was five and is currently living through her second global pandemic. Bertha grew up in a small house that sheltered nine children and two adults.

Bertha's brothers got sick, and before media or the World Health Organization was available with advice, Bertha's mom knew to keep the brothers quarantined in a boarded-up room away from the rest of the family.

Her mom entered and left the boys' room through a window, and she changed her clothes every time she left her sons, before she returned to the rest of the family.

More than 100 years ago, Bertha's astute mother understood the importance of physical distancing. She went to great lengths to keep her healthy family members safe. Today, more than 100 years later, Bertha has some advice to share: *Each person can do their part to help stop this pandemic from growing.*

Be kind to yourself and others. If you're alive in

2020, you get to choose. Will you be part of the problem or the solution? Will you do your part? Will you serve on the front lines? Can you stay home and stay safe? Social distancing can lead to the feeling of isolation, but it doesn't have to. There are a limitless number of ways you can connect to others and still be safe. People you love, people you know, and people you will never meet are counting on you.

We're all in this together. And those are more than just lyrics to a *High School Musical*.

Join the public Facebook group Social Distancing, An Extrovert's Survival Guide. There's a community waiting to connect with you.

SPECIAL THANKS

Thank you to my very talented cover artist, **Sheila Grace Page**. Shelia is a professional acrylic artist who teaches students of all ages and skill levels how to transform a blank canvas, or even just a sheet of paper, into a work of art. Sheila calls painting her medicine and says it calms her. One way she connects to others during a time of social distancing is through leading online painting classes. Sheila is available for virtual painting parties with your friends. Gather your friends online, pick a date and contact Sheila at better2getherunderpressure-@gmail.com. You can also connect with her on Facebook under Sheila Grace Page.

Thank you to my friend and former colleague, Dr. Raul Garcia for writing the forward. Raul is someone who believes in people, works to support our local community, inspires people to make small healthy changes, and walks his talk. As a physician, he supports healthy living, physically and mentally.

Thank you to my development editor, Bob Gerst, who guided my professional delivery, and who helped me better understand this journey through the eyes of an extrovert.

Thank you to my proofreader and lifelong friend, Kiann Jaeger. Through her example of kindness, she taught me 30 years ago what it means to be a good human.

Thank you to Rachel Hershberger, Laura Hefner, Whitney Stohr-Hendrickson, and Melea June Brown for sharing their personal stories, tips and recipes.

Thank you also to my many friends, clients and members of the public Facebook group **Social Distancing, An Extrovert's Survival Guide**, who trusted me with their obstacles and allowed me to coach them through creating a successful plan.

ABOUT THE AUTHOR

Debra Yergen is a bestselling author, public speaker, and certified life coach with a passion for helping. She specializes in corporate crisis communications, nonprofit strategic planning and board of directors development, as well as personal coaching clients through Olive Press Coaching. She is a graduate of the Washington State University, Edward R. Murrow School of Communications and the University of Washington, Foster School of Business. She trained in coaching and energy leadership through iPEC. Connect with her on Twitter @Debra_Yergen and @OlivePressCoach.

Other books by Debra:

Creating Job Security (series)

Creating Job Security Through Mobility and Diversity

Finding My Dazzle: A Zebra's Journey

Grace Knows Your Name: 30 Days of Thanksgiving

Real Life 101

Sweet Pickles Take Time: 12 Days of God's Love and Grandma's Recipes

The Eulogy (Book 1 in the Gift of Grace trilogy)

The Bench (Book 2 in the Gift of Grace trilogy)

The Gathering (Book 3 in the Gift of Grace trilogy)

Coming Spring 2021: Unexpected Blessings

For media interviews and public speaking bookings:
email: info@debrayergenco.com
Or call +1 509 910 6679